A celebration of
Britain's finest
hand coloured
textiles 1900-1994

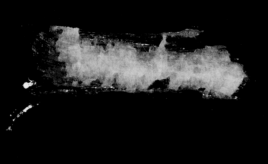

colour into Cloth

Contents

Portion of a lady's skirt, English or
French, 1730s, (detail)
Moiré silk; blockprinted with an
outline design, painted in colours
The Whitworth Art Gallery,
University of Manchester

I first encountered the blockprinted textiles of Barron and Larcher during a visit to the Crafts Study Centre, Bath, some years ago. I responded immediately to their strong graphic quality, and found the way the designs related to the folds of the furnishing lengths immensely satisfying. Later, again at the Crafts Study Centre, I also met the gentler cloths of Susan Bosence, and was equally enthralled. I was therefore delighted when Barley Roscoe, Curator of the Holburne Museum and Crafts Study Centre, agreed to collaborate on the exhibition 'Colour into Cloth' and this publication which accompanies it. 'Colour into Cloth' attempts to chart the development of hand-coloured textiles in Britain during the twentieth century, from the pioneering blockprinters and dyers – Barron and Larcher, Cryséde, Footprints and Enid Marx – to the many techniques used, often layer on layer, by the wide range of people working today. Our aim is to bring these individual makers to a wider public, and to encourage a greater appreciation of the different methods and marks they employ.

I am grateful to Margot Coatts, exhibition curator, and Linda Brassington, advisor, for their extensive research and attention to detail, and to Jennifer Harris, of the Whitworth Art Gallery, Manchester, for her generous assistance. We are particularly grateful to those institutions and individuals who have kindly loaned textiles, from their collections, enabling us to provide both an historical and international context.

We are also grateful to those who have given us technical and historical advice and assistance especially:

Sylvia Backermeyer, Howard Batho, Hazel Berriman, Hazel Clark, Jonathan Docherty, Anne Dolley, Helen Grundy, Rosemary Harden, Neil Harvey, Valerie Mendes, Mary Schoeser, Jennifer Wearden, Warners Fabrics.

We are especially grateful to the makers working currently for their enthusiasm and support, and for making both past and recent work available for the duration of the tour.

Foreword

Introduction

British printed, painted and dyed craft textiles of the 20th century by Margot Coatts (Exhibition Curator)

Piece, Japanese,
early 20th century (?)
Cotton; 'shibori' bound-resist patterned, dyed in indigo H40 W40
West Surrey College of Art and Design Textile Collection, [8090]; given by R & H Tanner 1988, originally from the Phyllis Barron Collection

The works in this publication, and the exhibition which it accompanies, are functional textiles, conceived as furnishings, clothing and accessories, or elements within architectural schemes; a small number operate as decorative wall-panels. The textiles, old and new, share the characteristic of being primarily concerned with the ways in which colour soaks into cloth, is resisted by barriers, and makes patterns in the process.

To introduce the exhibition, a small group of textiles has been selected from world sources – from Europe, Asia, India and Africa – simply to act as a series of signposts to the rich uses of colour in the textile arts. These pieces demonstrate how sophisticated colouring techniques, particular to certain regions, produce their own curiously self-imposed imagery.

In Britain this century extraordinary results have been achieved by individual craft workers, manipulating standard techniques or devising their own, from about 1920. There is little evidence of the existence of much individual textile printing activity in the twentieth century before the First World War, as compared with the 'revivals' in embroidery and hand-weaving which stirred before the turn of the century in various corners of the British Isles. Although William Morris's blockprinting and dyeing, practised from the 1880s until well into the twentieth century, was a clear forerunner, it was considered to be a form of 'manufacturing' – and therefore somewhat alien – by the early craft producers. Natural- or vegetable-dyeing, however, was developed in the small craft workshop by the hand-weaver Ethel Mairet and others from 1913 onwards.

The conventional route for artists or illustrators emerging from the art schools and wishing to go into printed textile design in the post-First World War period was to sell designs to

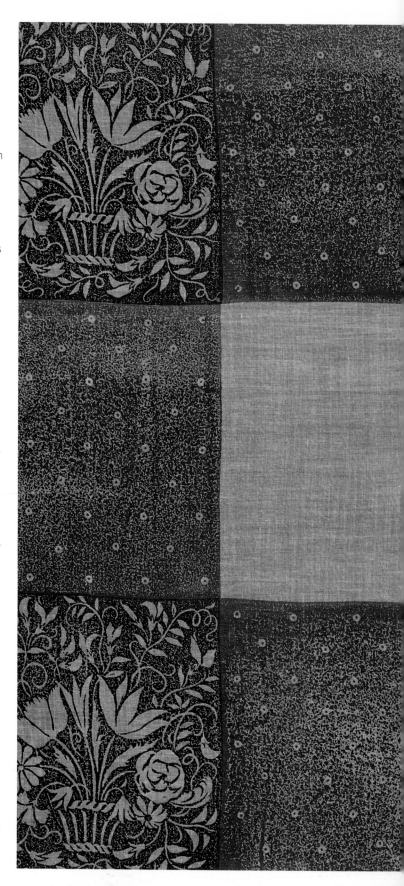

large firms like G.P. & J. Baker Ltd, the Silver Studio or Liberty's. Only a minority of them wanted to cut the blocks, or to discover and mix the dyes themselves: Phyllis Barron and Dorothy Larcher, Alec Walker at Cryséde, Joyce Clissold at Footprints and Enid Marx can be considered the main pioneers of the 'hands-on' approach. Although the work of each has its distinctive lino-block style, their work all displays the gusto of the Jazz Age combined with the rugged character of craft production.

During the next decade a few more fine artists, interested in either hand-blockprinted images or wax-resist patterning (batik), turned to textiles; these included Frank Dobson, E.Q. Nicholson and Nancy Nicholson. All three worked in a figurative vein, but devoted themselves to the production of textiles for only limited periods in their careers. Trained design graduates emerging from the Royal College of Art in the 1930s, such as Margaret Simeon and Marianne de Trey, quickly found a commercial market for their work; de Trey, however, wholly devoted her career to pottery from 1947.

At this period, yet another group of artists were commissioned to make designs for textiles by specialised commercial firms, such

Above: *Barron & Larcher*
Length of 'Girton', c.1924 (detail)
Linen; mordanated in tannic, blockprinted with iron on an undyed ground L251.5 W132
Crafts Study Centre, Holburne Museum, Bath

Left: *Margaret Simeon*
Piece of Furnishing Fabric, 1940s (details) Silk organza; blockprinted with dyes L95.5 W110.5
The Whitworth Art Gallery

as Allan Walton Textiles or Edinburgh Weavers. These artists were not the executants of the textiles, and thus fall outside the remit of this publication.

After the Second World War the concept of design for industry held sway. A new scale and style – large, bold and flat – entered printed textiles. It often incorporated hand-drawn or roughly textured 'arty' motifs in black, loosely superimposed over abstract coloured shapes or plain grounds. Such patterns, printed by photo-silkscreen by the leading firms, almost replaced the desire for real craft-printed textiles, which all but disappeared from view.

The 1960s saw renewed energy and interest begin to return to the crafts in Britain. In textiles, the few practitioners who had continued to print by hand-block were regarded as nothing short of mild eccentrics, but Joyce Clissold in her Brentford workshop attracted many student visitors and Susan Bosence's gentle fabrics and teaching work at Dartington's Adult Education Centre gained recognition.

Contemporary architecture increased in scale and, to decorate it, the one-off wall-hanging, both woven and painted, rose in popularity. Noel Dyrenforth's abstract batik panels or paintings were one example of a genre in which individual works became sought after. This was due in part to their inclusion in 'The Craftsman's Art' exhibition (CAC at the V&A, 1972) and the increase of contemporary craft exhibitions in public museums and galleries generally. A leading maker of such works since the 1970s is the quilter-dyer Diana Harrison, who in retrospect can be seen as an early activist in a line of cloth colourists which also includes Sally Greaves-Lord and Rushton Aust. Increasingly these last two contemporary makers work to commission for specific sites.

Furnishing for private houses, particularly for period schemes, is an area in which the craft textile producer is occasionally involved. Cressida Bell, as well as producing stylish scarves, has carried out such schemes recently and Lesley Sunderland has made a contribution over the last 15 years. Fluent drawing is the basis of this form of textile design, together with a knowledge of decorative styles and dramatic colourways. Bell's medium is screenprinting while Sunderland prints by wood-block or paints directly onto cloth.

The tide had turned towards useful, wearable craft textiles by the early 1980s and they became an increasingly important part of the fashion world. Early leaders were Georgina von Etzdorf and Sian Tucker, working in screenprinting and hand-painting respectively. Younger makers, including Kate Blee, Neil Bottle, Trisha Needham, Victoria Richards and Sharon Ting, have followed this path, using printing, painting and discharging techniques conventionally and in unusual combinations, on silks and wools. Interesting and varied ground cloths are an important feature of craft production.

It is not surprising that, partly in reaction to the type of pattern which can be produced by screen and block, certain makers have remained close to the painterly approach. Sally Greaves-Lord and Sian Tucker were amongst the first modern textile practitioners to recognise painted flat pattern on flexible cloth as their natural medium, whilst others – Dawn Dupree, Noel Dyrenforth, Norma Starszakowna and Carole Waller – use the medium in various ways for compositions based on narrative imagery, often incorporating spatial illusion. It is in this area of the craft that the capacities of liquid colour on a flat piece of cloth are seen tested to the limits.

Susan Bosence:
An interview with
Barley Roscoe

Interview

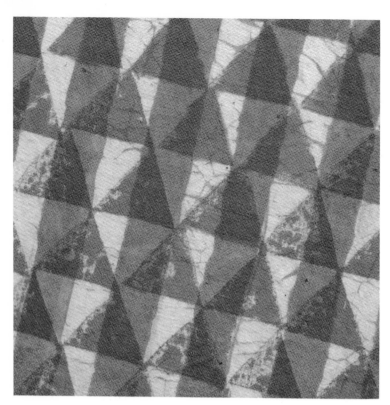

Susan Bosence
Length of 'Triangles', 1991 (detail)
Cotton; blockprinted with iron rust,
flour paste resist L206 W102
Crafts Council Collection

"I feel that my work has got something more than just making patterns. It's part of a vision or an excitement, something you only catch on the wind of fleeting things, something you can't explain and you don't know where it comes from…"

Hand-blockprinting and the resist-dyeing of textiles, both for dress and domestic furnishing, have formed an integral part of Susan Bosence's life now for over forty years and she finds her craft quite compulsive. "I'm really interested in the mark a block can make and how near you can get to whatever this inspiration is, this bit of magic, and try to transform it… and put it onto… just the right type of cloth… the silk, the wool… the diaphanous bit of georgette… and achieve the design which looks as though it belongs to it…. It almost equals the thrill of rubber gloves and indigo, of sloshing about with this marvellous colour and working with other people… and we've had some wonderful days with a vat… Rust is pretty seductive too…".

Susan Bosence's childhood did not suggest the happiness and pleasure she has enjoyed later in life. Born in Luton, the eldest of two girls, her mother was a Quaker and her father owned a factory "responsible for making an enormous variety of patterns for straw hats". An early memory associated with a craft is of watching her grandmother plait straw by hand. Susan Bosence entered the local high school where she "had a horrible time" and "was a bit of a rebel". Sustained by her Aunt Rose, who saved her "from a lot of unhappiness", her artistic talent remained unnourished by her parents who "were sort of left over Victorians. They were far too strict and, well, misunderstanding".

On leaving school, having finally passed her maths for School Certificate on the third attempt, an exchange to a Swiss family in Geneva proved a marvellous release and marked "the beginning of the happy part of my life". Here, apart from enjoying the Lake and winter sports and improving her French, she had the opportunity to work in Jean Piaget's office, a department of the International Bureau of Education, where she learnt about schools and educationists who had a more enlightened philosophy of education.

With the Second World War looming Susan returned to England and started work for the New Education Fellowship, "an important and strong movement in the educational world". Through this group she attended summer schools and conferences at Dartington, a progressive and artistic community fostered by Dorothy and Leonard Elmhirst in the heart of the Devon countryside. Subsequently she went to live there when invited to become secretary for Bill Curry, the headmaster of the "most wonderful school you could possibly have wished for".

After the War and "surrounded by all the beauty of Dartington" Susan Bosence felt compelled to start making "something myself". An invitation to tea by Dorothy Elmhirst to see Barron and Larcher's "gorgeous printed cottons" proved to show her "just exactly what I thought I wanted to do… I was very inspired… and I bought some fabric printing inks from Dryad's, very expensive so I could only afford two colours and this restriction over expense has been with me all the time.." Dorothy Elmhirst was very supportive and suggested she consult Muriel Rose, then Crafts Officer with the British Council. Acknowledging Susan Bosence showed "real talent for textile design" despite "a lack of technique", Muriel Rose continued to see her two or three times a year, and "she would give me a really hard, hurting tutorial on what I was doing, so I feel I had a jolly good start by having her as a mentor…". In 1951 through Rose, she received an invitation to Barron and

Larcher's home in the Cotswolds. She warmed to both women and responded instantly to the feast of hand-blockprinted textiles she was shown and the beauty of their home, especially the garden, which Barron tended – "I used to just devour every sight of her garden…She had a most exquisite collection of beautiful flowers, plants… the ones that touched me most were the very delicate ones with fine, fine lines – starting fine and then just going off into nothingness, and wonderful little spots in exactly the right place, and all this, you know, I absorbed, and I couldn't stop thinking about them and I think it came through in my work…"

Phyllis Barron was soon to become a close friend and support, encouraging Susan Bosence's early prints of simplified stars and flowers and spots and stripes, and seeming almost relieved to pass on her knowledge and expertise. She made a special trip to

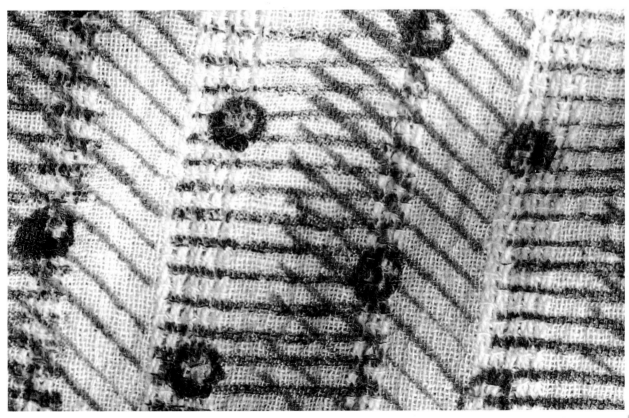

stay with Susan and the Bosence family and showed her how to make an indigo vat, a favourite dye that Susan was also to find compulsive. Susan Bosence feels that, together, Barron and Larcher almost perfected the art of printing and over-printing using blocks, acknowledging that their fine art training stood them in good stead in their designs. She recognises drawing to be important to some fabric printers but feels "I have usually been able to say what I want to say directly with the block and cutter". She is skilled at refining a deceptively simple pattern from a complex image. The idea for a horizontal and diagonal pattern of lines with spots was distilled from a visit to "a tiny little mountain village church (in France)... There were bars at the windows and the light was coming through the bars onto a textured floor. I think... there was some lace in it as well, but it was the play of the intensity of the light coming through these bars, the density of those, their power to stop the light coming through , and yet (at) the same time the delicacy that you get from fineness... that sparked this design."

In the finished cloth Susan Bosence strives to capture the very essence of a particular place or moment in the design, colour and texture and draws on "those connections... associations with sight... a vision of something, a remembrance..." to do so. She has also added immensely to her range, by embracing other forms of resist-dyeing in various combinations, including trailed wax and paste, stitching, pleating and folding methods.... Her colour schemes reflect Dartmoor where she lives but "if we decided to live in France... I think the whole palette would change. The intensity of the sun and colours in the flowers, and so on, are in another world... from the softness and subtlety of Devon...".

Teaching has played an important part in her life and provided a stimulus to her own work. Helping to set up the Adult Education Centre at Dartington in the 1960s, where she taught part-time, was her first teaching experience; this was also a great help when she planned her own workshop at Sigford in 1966. "The work bound us all together and we got so involved in it... teaching is really a form of sharing, of handing over and exchanging ideas and, well, growing as you go along..." She was also to teach in art colleges at Farnham and Camberwell – "I was always doing a bit of teaching, partly because I really loved it and it seemed to be part of my life, – being bound up with other artists – and partly because we needed the money".

A highly successful exhibition in the Ceylon Tea Centre, London, in 1961 launched Susan Bosence's career and as result she "never really had to look around for the next commission or next thing to do because there was always something waiting to be done". More exhibitions were to follow in Bristol, Dartington and Bath, offering a rhythm of working that could be happily adopted. At the same time the 1961 exhibition also offered a choice for it was "a great big boot of a send off. I didn't know whether I was on my head or my heels.... Invitations...and orders (came) from all over and had I been a different kind of person I could have developed it into a whizz-bang concern, I think, because there was terrific interest in it, but I didn't want to be an administrator, an organiser, I wanted to do it myself. And I wanted to get into the wonderful, magical world of (Barron's) garden, and the spots and the marks I wanted to make and the designs I wanted to do: I just wanted to be mixed up with all that side of it". It was entirely characteristic that Susan decided to remain true to herself.

Sally Greaves-Lord:
a crafts-woman of our
time – taken from
conversations and letters
in 1993/94
by Margot Coatts

Interview

The first thing Sally Greaves-Lord told me about herself was that, even from childhood, she liked cloth; from the moment she went to art college, she loved it. Her art education is still dominant in her mind, despite having left the Royal College of Art over 12 years ago and West Surrey College of Art (Farnham) two years before that.

Arriving on the textiles course at Farnham in 1977, Greaves-Lord was anxious to find her metier. "Farnham has all these little courses but I opted for printed textiles. I was dying to get colour – pattern – onto cloth." She evolved a technique which suited her, a combination of painting and screenprinting. At the time there was very little "real hand-painting" going on in British textiles, making the direction she took seem quite new.

In the summer holiday, at the end of the second college year, Greaves-Lord went alone to Vienna; she relished all of the city and its art. Originally, her intention had been just to seek out the work of the painter Friedensreich Hundertwasser, whose artist's books she had enjoyed in England. His work had a seminal influence with that of other Viennese artists; she returned to college with a new resolve and direction.

Greaves-Lord found that being taught, "having to be good at things", had become a burden but by the third year, she recollects, this feeling left her. A new independence gave her confidence – "I had this image in my mind of exactly what I wanted to put on cloth" – and for the first time she felt "completely on course". The habit of forming a near-complete mental image before beginning a textile work has stayed with her ever since.

By the mid-1980s Greaves-Lord's near-monochrome painting and discharging technique for darkly coloured silk banners

had become her signature. How did it evolve? "That happened at the Royal College of Art. The stuff I had done at Farnham was all neater, by comparison; at the RCA everything changed". She found the Royal College almost too exciting, and so set herself the discipline of working with just two colours, using Procion dyes on cotton. As a result, her works became more concerned with the compositional elements than with the interaction of colour: "They were all about obscuring things, or they were balances." The development of the process was far from a textbook exercise: "You stumble across new things that happen but they are reasonably difficult to control. The environment, the steaming, how much you wrap the cloth up, I assume these make the differences."

The learning curve was not just in technical matters: "I think perhaps I had fears that I couldn't use colour anyway, so I used mainly black and blue, and anything that could be derived from them by bleaching out. I concentrated on that to the exclusion of anything else for two years." She applied the dyes by painting, stencilling and also screenprinting in large areas, the scale of the work being "very heavy and monumental… even oppressive, looking back at it".

On leaving the RCA, Greaves-Lord was aware that she did not really like the city but, curiously, she stayed in London for another eight years. At first she sold fabric prototypes for commercial prints, renting space in Diana Harrison's studio. At that period she went quite frequently to Edinburgh to make drawings; they too contained no colour – "just ink and paper and big". Drawing, at that stage, was a matter of learning to handle the brush or pencil and not, as in her landscapes of the last few years, an expression of personal feeling.

Sally Greaves-Lord
Scarf from the 'Lavender Grey' series, 1989 (detail)
Spun silk; painted with dyes and discharge L137 W45

Then came her first important commission for a painted interior, from Research Recordings through the architect Pierre Davoine in 1983. It was a mural in a double-height reception area in Camden Town. "I had never done any large-scale painting before, I still get feelings of shock when I begin jobs and I think, how am I going to do that?" This was the beginning of a string of work in conjunction with architects Powell Tuck Connor and Orefelt Ltd.

In her studio it was a fertile time. She made silk banners and painted floor mats; exhibitions of these at Contemporary Applied Arts, in 1986 and '88, sold out. During these years at least half her energy was devoted to painted interiors and working, from 1985, for Issey Miyake UK as creative director. The displays at the new Issey Miyake shop in Sloane Street were her sole responsibility. Alison Britton, in her introductory essay accompanying the 1988 exhibition at Contemporary Applied Arts, defined Greaves-Lord's strength in a few words: "The interior, all of it, is her subject."

Sally Greaves-Lord's reputation has grown in tandem with the architectural commissions which, in turn, have exploited her natural talent for working on a very large scale. While her contemporaries and studio partners were busy selling designs for scarves and accessories, Greaves-Lord was painting yet more interiors and banners. Glenn Sujo of Art Guidelines has involved her in some challenging projects, including a a pair of hangings commissioned for the art collection of Arthur Andersen and Co in 1990. The importance of this project was that it signalled Greaves-Lord's breakthrough into hotter colours. She continued this line of enquiry with works for the 1990 promotional exhibition, seen only in Japan, 'Great British Design', organised by the design partnership Pentagram. Despite the sea-change to a

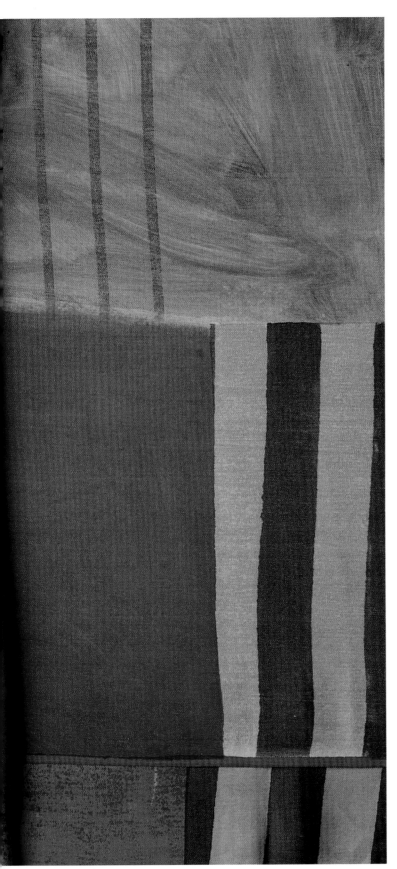

more light-hearted range of reds and ambers, she passed over this significant stage of the work lightly as "almost like the old compositions with the new colours".

Reducing her own palette to the level of a trade paint card is typical of Sally Greaves-Lord's self-deprecatory attitude but it does not do justice to these arresting and dynamic works of the 1990s. Since moving to a village in the bracing hinterland of Scarborough, Yorkshire, she has been making a good many smaller things "just for decoration's sake" and has also changed the format of the ground cloth to a wider rectangle or a square. With recent work spread out in front of her, she reflected: "I used to think that decoration had such meaning and strength and symbols, and I felt that I had been searching to find my own symbols. For ages I just made myself use straight lines, rectangles, stripes and dots ('keep it simple!') and I always hated other people's insensitivity to [the vocabularies of] decoration".

The latest textiles are painted from both sides. Two or three motifs are overlayed on one side, then the cloth is steamed and washed, then painted in a mirror image from the reverse; soaked and streaked areas can be interrelated, front and back. The method was a necessary evolution when working in a shared studio during her last year in London; the discharge process was voted "smelly and offensive" and was duly dropped.

Amongst Greaves-Lord's most pleasing recent works (1992-3) are a dozen or more scarves, a personal collection from which she picks her daily wardrobe. They contain favourite colours and the decorative 'code' of spots, broken strokes and curves, painted on both sides yet seeming to come from inside the cloth. These scarves, worked within tight boundaries, are maquettes to map the directions which lead to major works. Looking at a green one, and in answer to nagging questions about the sources of her colour, Greaves-Lord ventured wryly, "It's very grassy, very foliage."

It is tempting to classify the smallest works, asymmetrically shaped silk fragments made as artwork for Issey Miyake's printed cards, as minor pieces. They are not; they are complete ideas in a somewhat reduced 'code', using rapid brush strokes of integrated colours. Like the large works, they are spontaneous within the limitations of the medium (acid dyes on silk). "I know the feeling a particular piece has to have, then I will draw a small diagram in a sketchbook, no bigger than A5... The colour comes last, usually". She begins to paint on the cloth in the knowledge of "just what suits the piece", putting down the certainties of colour first. A working method has now been set in motion in which Greaves-Lord will stand and reflect, then work very rapidly. She must paint, discharge, wash out and steam almost in a state of suspense before learning just what her reactions and reflections have produced on the cloth this time.

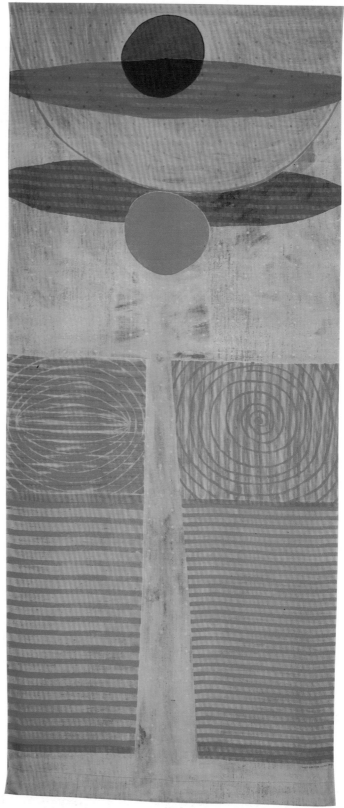

Sally Greaves-Lord
Banner 'Pink and Orange Spirals', 1991; Spun silk; painted with dyes front and back L213 W92

Georgina von Etzdorf:
An interview
with Jennifer Harris

Interview

The silks, velvets and wools for which Georgina von Etzdorf has acquired an enviable reputation in the fashion world over the past decade are hand-screenprinted in surroundings which would be highly familiar to anyone working for a small craft-based company. All of the main production and finishing processes are carried out on two floors of a converted barn at Odstock in Wiltshire, complete with a Heath Robinson-ish steamer constructed from old oil drums and cheek by jowl with the marketing and merchandising side of the operation. Only the lines of boxes containing samples of the new season's designs and labelled for Frankfurt, Paris, Milan, Tokyo and New York hint at the international scope of the organisation.

The contacts with stores and buyers abroad were made early in the company's life. After taking a degree in textile design, where she specialised in print because of her interest in painting, which she still does as a hobby, Georgina von Etzdorf tried selling designs to the industry, but with only limited success:

"I knew that the designs themselves were too individual, they said too much about me and not, perhaps, enough about current trends in the textile industry."

The present company was formed in 1981 in partnership with Jonathan Docherty and Martin Simcock, fellow graduates of Camberwell School of Art. The arrangement has proved mutually supportive, allowing Georgina von Etzdorf to concentrate on designing and personally promoting their collections, whilst Jonathan Docherty and Martin Simcock are responsible for marketing and merchandising respectively. As early as 1982 they were exporting their work to the USA, selling through Bergdorf Goodman in New York. Having learnt that there were buying officers representing the major stores abroad and whose job it was to scout out

Georgina von Etzdorf
Regular Wrap 'Rosamundi', 1993
(detail) Silk chiffon with satin stripe;
screenprinted in blended colours
with dyes, hand-rolled edges
L175 W105

new talent, they quickly set up appointments to meet buyers, many of whom showed interest. It was also in 1982 that they took part in their first trade exhibition, at the Paris fashion shows, and the partnership now takes its two annual collections both to the Paris men's – and women's wear shows. It is an interesting fact that, from the beginning, the company was making more sales abroad than in the UK and indeed continues to be export-led, with sales abroad accounting annually for 65-70% of the total, although it is important to remember that the export figure does cover a number of major markets.

Although it has been a factor, the link with the fashion industry cannot account solely for the company's success. There is only a limited range of classic garments – such as simple tunics, luxurious pyjamas and dressing gowns, and von Etzdorf devotees are highly diverse in age and background. The company has received a great deal of publicity recently for its printed velvets, which fit in so well with the current mood of fashion, but printed velvets have appeared annually in their collections since 1985 and will probably continue to do so. "Every now and again", says Georgina von Etzdorf, "our vision happens to coincide with something currently very fashionable, but our aim, when producing a collection, is to look for a new direction or challenge for ourselves. Because we work within the fashion field we naturally have to be aware of how it is developing, but the fundamental drive comes from us."

In addition to the success of the velvets, turnover has been steadily improving as a result of the increased visibility given to their products by the opening up of a number of sales outlets. The first London shop was opened in Burlington Arcade in 1986, the second in Sloane Street in 1988. At Barneys on Madison Avenue in New York there is a Georgina von Etzdorf shop within the store.

All three provide an opportunity for each new collection to be seen as a whole, something which the designer regards as important.

The commercial success of Georgina von Etzdorf inevitably begs the question as to why not take the step of moving from hand to mechanical production and thereby increase output and reduce prices to reach a larger section of the market? Having rejected at the outset the idea of sending their designs out to be printed because a factory would claim that something could not be done or could be done only if a huge minimum order was placed, Georgina von Etzdorf sees no reason to go back on that decision:

"Unless you've got someone who is working for you almost exclusively and who believes in what you're doing it's very difficult to demand certain experimental techniques, such as turning the screen round or adding something to the dyes to achieve different effects."

She is firmly of the belief that printing by hand rather than by machine allows them to achieve effects which simply could not be achieved any other way, because you cannot so easily stop the process to intervene:

"In hand-printing you can change elements; as you're going along you can develop and adapt or monitor the quality of what you're producing. You can always push it a bit further."

Techniques involve painting on to both screen and fabric in addition to screenprinting but whilst they remain constantly aware that any effects must be reproducible, commercial considerations do not take priority:

"If you're always under those constraints (i.e. to be commercially viable), you can stop the

Georgina von Etzdorf
Waistcoat 'Cypher', 1993 (detail)
Silk jacquard; screenprinted in stripes with dyes; bounded edges to pockets, and covered pockets L58

most wonderful things from happening. We often have things in the collection which take ages to produce, but yet they're not costed in much higher than anything else because it's an experiment, we're seeing how they work and whether we can develop the idea."

Not surprisingly, Georgina von Etzdorf herself must work closely with the printers in the early stages of the production process, although her own rôle within the company is now clearly defined as Artistic Director.

Georgina von Etzdorf and her two studio assistants come up with designs for two collections a year. The men's wear collection generally includes about eleven designs in five to six different colourways, and the women's wear around six designs in the same number of colourways. There are some designs common to both and, occasionally, an old design may be re-introduced and re-coloured, if it seems appropriate to that collection. A design usually begins as a watercolour drawing, but invariably changes and evolves. Sometimes it will be used in its original form and simply put into the appropriate repeat size but, more often, elements are extracted and photocopied and the photocopies themselves then drawn into. Rarely now is the finished design completely painted out, and the screen-makers are able to work from something which is part painted, part photocopied, redrawn and often in several layers. Georgina von Etzdorf characterises the company's designs as organic and rhythmical, abstract though loosely based on natural forms. What makes them so distinctive is her use of colour which is intended to convey resonances of particular times of day, weather or other natural phenomena.

The company continues to expand gradually and looks to the future with optimism. Immediate plans involve moving the

Georgina von Etzdorf
Regular Wrap 'Rosamundi', 1993
(detail) Silk chiffon with satin stripe;
screenprinted in blended clours
with dyes, hand-rolled edges
L175 W105

production side of the business into a new building with more room for the printing, leaving the existing barn for sales, administration generally and design. Whilst the three partners think vaguely of moving into other products, "We always remember how we started in this and what a hard slog it's been. If we do go into other areas we want to have a clear understanding of what we're trying to do and how."

Sharon Ting:
An Interview with
Linda Brassington

Sharon Ting's reference file of scarves and banners is evidence of her creative energy and prolific productivity since graduating from the Royal College of Art in 1992.

In her early days as a student at Wimbledon, Ting's painting focused on colour and texture. This led her to specialise in textiles at the West Surrey College of Art and Design. "I always knew that I wanted to make... my introduction to both print and weave at Farnham confirmed that. Although I wanted that kind of activity, I rarely felt fulfilled by my work. Very late in the course, I was still in a muddle – even convinced that I wanted to make hats at one point! My tutors encouraged me to return to my painting. . That was the turning point." The results were banners in which she sensitively translated her colourful compositions into cloth.

At the Royal College of Art, Ting learned how to retain her creative identity within industrial design projects. The initial emphasis on paper design was a difficult adjustment. "I used to sneak into the print room in the evenings and just develop ideas on cloth, sampling around the project." Eventually, Ting confronted the challenge to develop her work *through* the projects. Once again, she immersed herself in her painting, but this time applying her print techniques to paper. "I tore paper, I made paper, I collaged with different papers; I printed on them at different stages as if they were cloth; layering colour and surfaces onto paper to create tactile qualities."

Ting was able to design with comparative ease, experiencing professional practice in a commercial studio in New York and selling designs internationally. Her fluency on paper built her a strong portfolio but her desire to print remained. She values the breadth of her experience, however. "Economically, it's essential to be versatile. I'm no longer scared of industry and I don't see it as something separate from my work." Manufacturers are now interested in her ideas on cloth and are keen to find ways of reproducing them industrially. 'Firifis' are currently developing a collection of furnishing fabrics incorporating her work. Ting's subtle discharge effects are being carefully interpreted with alternative processes. These are now resolved and will go into production shortly. The range, to be launched at London's exhibition of furnishings, 'Decorex' in 1994, exploits Ting's double-layered look, with sheers and opaques working together on a wide range of cottons and silks.

Commissions, usually for her banners, are an important aspect of production. These come about largely through exhibitions but also through the work of her agents who seek them out and assist in their smooth operation. "Commissions are very hard to get. When I exhibited at 'Interior Design International', I spent hours noting the names and addresses of interested people and then tried to follow them up. It takes a long time; and then, once the commission is under way, so many people are involved – the landlord, the architect, the builder. My agents provide support through the whole procedure."

Ting's scarves developed from her banners. Attempts to achieve her double-layered look on a different fabric led her to the process of devoré, and velvet fitted in with new fashion developments. The demand from retailers is regular and each order finances the next. Produced in batches, each scarf is open to some variation. The cloth is masked and painted in layers of colour. A screen is employed to provide definition and structure, and discharge is applied to achieve changes in tone. The results are assessed and, if necessary, further layers are built up "until they are right". Usually an order can take up to a month to complete but it is

important, between production, to allocate time and 'space' for fresh thoughts. Buyers will invite her to present new collections but these need to show developments.

Each new range begins with a palette of colour; as many as twenty new print pastes form the basis of her work. Currently, devoré is a key element but Ting is able to manipulate a broad range of processes that will extend and develop her textiles in the future. Does she have a five-year plan? "Well, I have a two-year plan to make my work known abroad". In little more than a year, Ting's work has reached major British retailers and galleries. The cycle of orders and exhibitions has already been established here but, as international trade fairs, publications and touring exhibitions feature the work of Sharon May Yee Peng Ting, demand from new horizons seems imminent.

Sharon Ting
Long Scarf, 1993
Silk viscose velvet; dyed, painted with colour discharges, devoré-screenprinted L127 W51.5

Biographies

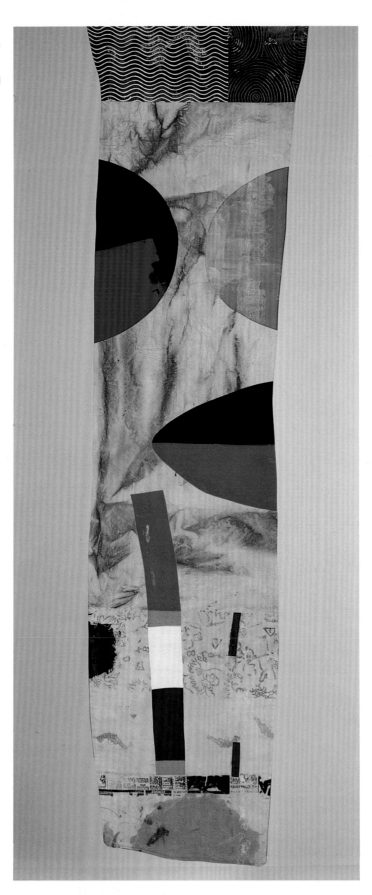

Rushton Aust
b.1958, Oxford, England
Rushton Aust trained in general textile design at Derby College of Art in the mid-1970s and then at the Royal College of Art, specialising in printed textiles. After graduating in 1981, he spent four years designing commercial prints for fashion market clients, including Jean Muir. Simultaneously, he travelled extensively in Japan and the Soviet Union, drawing inspiration for his work.

Aust set up his workshop in 1985, with the help of a Crafts Council Setting-Up Grant, moving to larger premises in Greenwich, south-east London, in 1993. Here he is equipped with a 5-metre print table which has enabled him to extend the scale of the banner-like hangings for which he is known. Much of Aust's work comes from commissions from clients requiring large-scale, wall- or free-hanging works for interiors; the textiles perform an architectural function. Several stages of close consultation with the architect and client are behind each piece.

The making of works for exhibition is an exploratory process which is paced differently; one piece can take anything from a few months to two years. For both commissioned and speculative work, images are absorbed into the cloth using a combination of dip-dyeing, spraying, painting and screen-printing (using photo-silkscreen methods and cut paper stencils). Pieces of cloth, variously patterned by these means, are stitched together in individual compositions (some of them tubular), which can also incorporate fragments of commercially printed textiles. Aust works from ideas developed in sketchbooks and collages, incorporating various things seen: landscapes, discarded fragments from the natural world and manufactured products.

Barron & Larcher

Phyllis Barron b.1890, London, died 1964, Painswick; Dorothy Larcher b.1884, died 1952, Painswick

The blockprinters Phyllis Barron and Dorothy Larcher were active between the two world wars. Both women had been trained as painters at art school: Barron at the Slade under Tonks, and Larcher at Hornsey School of Art.

Barron first became interested in printing on discovering some woodblocks in France when a student; she began to print in her Hampstead studio in about 1915, teaching herself empirically to use dyes. Contemporaneously, Larcher was working in India and saw blockprinters at work there; after meeting Barron on her return, she joined the workshop in 1923.

By then at 2 Parkhill Studios, Hampstead, they produced printed cottons, linens, velvets and silks using natural dyes for positive prints and also the discharge technique; blocks were cut in wood or lino. In 1930 Barron and Larcher moved to Painswick, Gloucestershire, where they bought a house with outbuildings and set up a workshop, dyehouse and a large indigo vat. From this time they integrated synthetic dyes into their work. Three assistants were regularly employed.

Barron and Larcher worked for many private clients to create furnishings and dress fabric; artists and craftsmen especially patronised them. Major commissions included furnishing fabric for the Duke of Westminster's 40-cabin yacht 'The Flying Cloud',

Detmar Blow's Gloucestershire house 'Hilles', the Fellows' senior common room at Girton College, Cambridge, and the choir stalls of Winchester Cathedral. They continued printing until wartime shortages defeated them, after which Larcher turned increasingly to flower painting and Barron to local government work, parish affairs and the occasional teaching assignment.

Cressida Bell

b.1959, Newcastle, England

After a foundation course at Middlesex Polytechnic and a BA at St Martin's College of Art, London, in fashion and textile design, Cressida Bell attended the Royal College of Art from 1982 to '84. Following graduation, and with the benefit of a Crafts Council Setting-Up Grant, she formed her first workshop in Hackney, moving to larger premises in the same district in 1989.

Working with partner Christine Miles, Cressida Bell hand-screenprints two collections of fashion textile accessories per year as well as cushions and furnishing fabrics; the studio uses a wide range of silks, wools and cottons. Bell is the author of the patterns, of which full-size paper designs exist, coloured with emulsion paints. These are vigorously drawn and have explored, over the last decade, a gamut of borders and repeats, large and small patterns, figurative and abstract motifs. The sources include the painted pottery of the Mediterranean and decorative features which she has found in architecture, costume and textiles whilst travelling. The more complex designs have necessitated up to five colour separations, but two or three is now more common. Colours are usually printed on a dyed ground, which is sometimes discharge-printed.

Exhibitions have figured in Bell's career since 1984, including those with her artist-family and others. Varied commissions have been undertaken including designs for commercially produced furnishing fabrics, tiles, carpets, museum scarves, room sets, letterheads and a book jacket.
(See illustration overleaf)

Philippa Bergson

b.1954, Surrey, England

After taking a BA course in embroidery at Manchester Polytechnic, Bergson attended the Royal College of Art, graduating in textiles in 1977. She set up a workshop at 401½ studios, London, painting and stitching silk cushions, scarves and lengths, while also teaching at three London art colleges and participating in group exhibitions.

Moving to Suffolk in 1985 and setting up a workshop in a wooden barn in her garden brought new patterns into the work; many of her present scarf designs are inspired by the countryside and the special East Anglian light. She sells these at East Anglian exhibitions and UK craft galleries.

Bergson has consistently concentrated on hand-painting on silk using the wax-resist method. The first stage is to paint on the ground colour, like a watercolour wash. The wax 'drawing' or design is then trailed or dripped onto the textile using traditional batik equipment; further motifs may be over-painted. Finally the cloth is steamed, washed, rinsed and drycleaned, to remove the wax.

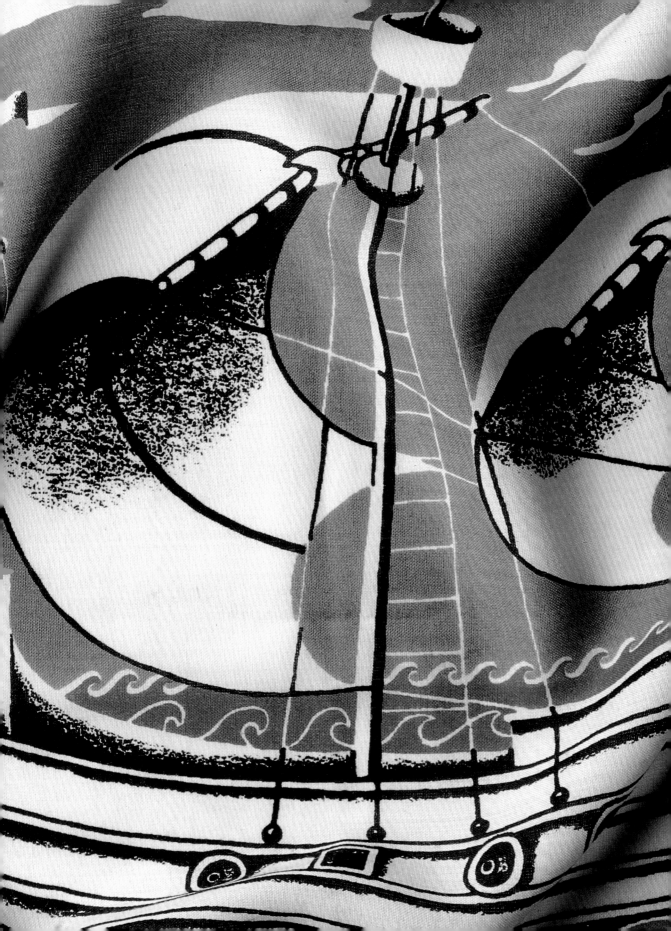

Kate Blee

b.1961, London

Kate Blee took a BA in printed textiles and a post-graduate diploma in design at Edinburgh College of Art, completing her studies in 1984. During this time she travelled to India on an Andrew Grant Scholarship. In 1986 she opened a workshop in Shoreditch with the help of a Crafts Council Setting-Up grant, and now operates from her studio in North London.

Her work explores simple painted shapes and areas of brushwork in which colour is ground into the cloth. She produces fashion accessories including wraps, ties and scarves in wool and silk, 'blanket paintings' and throws in thick wool cloth. When constructing a throw, several painted pieces of cloth are pieced together to form a composition.

Blee regularly undertakes commissions for carpets, rugs and runners, to be made in Turkey, and gouache designs for these fill many sketchbooks.

Blee's work is sold through selected London fashion shops and galleries, exhibitions and open studio events.

Susan Bosence

b.1913, Bedfordshire, England

Susan Bosence started her working life at the New Education Fellowship in London, moving to the post of headmaster's secretary in 1939 at Dartington Hall School, part of the estate in Devon owned by the enlightened Dorothy and Leonard Elmhirst.

Bosence's introduction to blockprinted textiles was through seeing examples from the 1920s and '30s by Barron and Larcher (see p.33) in the Elmhirsts' home and, while raising a family, she began to print fabrics for domestic use. In 1950 a visit to Phyllis Barron and Dorothy Larcher in the Cotswolds was arranged; Barron encouraged Bosence when she first set out and continued to advise her. Her earliest experiments were centred on resist-dyeing, combining wax and stitch-resists on cotton with indigo dye. Blockprinting

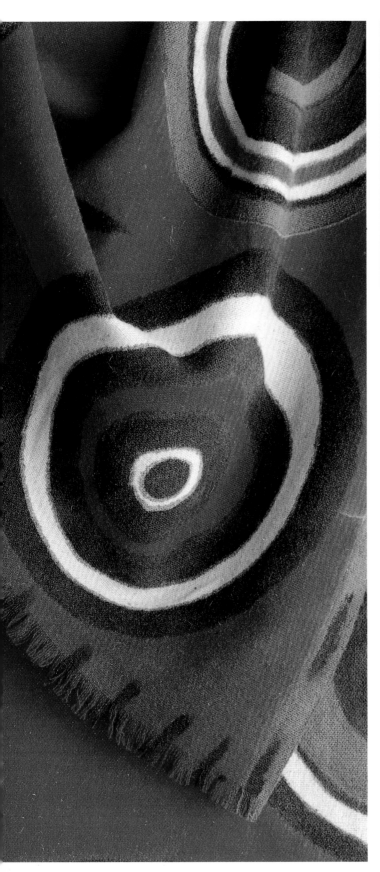

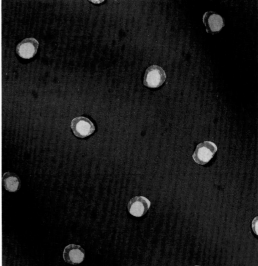

developed gradually; the early lino-printed patterns were often two simple but opposing blocks, such as a dot and a textured bar.

In the 1960s Bosence planned and opened a dyehouse and classroom for teaching at the Adult Education Centre, Dartington. Here she ran classes and also carried out her own work in collaboration with Annette Morel.

In 1966, Bosence moved to her present home; a farmhouse with a workshop in a converted barn in Devon; she continued to develop her affinity with dyestuffs, both natural and chemical, and with their uses within the textile arts. A successful exhibition at the Ceylon Tea Centre, London, in 1961 brought numerous private commissions and part-time teaching jobs at art colleges. These defined the pattern of Bosence's life for the next 15 years. For the last decade, Bosence has worked alone, assisted by Heather Williams and others when preparing for exhibitions.

In 1985 Susan Bosence published *Hand Block Printing and Resist Dyeing*.

Neil Bottle
b. 1966, Ramsgate, England
Neil Bottle moved into his London studio and began exhibiting at crafts and design fairs immediately after graduation from Middlesex

Above: *Susan Bosence*
Length of 'Oman',
1990-91, (detail)
Fine poplin; blockprinted,
wax-resist patterned and
over-dyed L259 W91.5
Crafts Council Collection

Left: *Kate Blee*
Long Scarf 'Targets',
1993 (detail) Wool;
painted with dyes on
both sides; cut fringe
L264 W74

Neil Bottle
Panel 'Burnt Orange
Geometric', 1993
(detail) Silk dupion;
painted, stencilled and
screenprinted with dyes
and pigments
L200 W57

Polytechnic in 1989. In 1991 a Crafts Council Setting-Up Grant enabled him to convert a large, well-equipped workshop in Ramsgate, Kent; here he now works with Julia Bottle, his wife, and two assistants.

The workshop produces accessories on silk as well as hanging panels on silk dupion. For all these, a combination of hand-screenprinting and painting are carried out in repeated operations. Photographically reproduced line images, usually printed in black, are derived from Bottle's pen-and-ink drawings or linocuts; other graphic sources include 'borrowed' lettering and calligraphy, maps and plans. Sixty colours are mixed to the workshop's recipes and sometimes worked 'wet on wet' for special effects.

Neil Bottle evolves new collections each year but does not adhere strictly to fashion seasons. He also makes hanging panels for exhibition or to commission; examples of the latter have recently been acquired by the Victoria and Albert Museum and the Cooper Hewitt Museum, New York.

Crysède – Alec Walker

b. 1889, Mirfield, Yorkshire, England; died 1964, Falmouth, England
Alec Walker came from a Yorkshire textile family and entered the family business. In 1912, aged 23, his father gave him a small mill from which he produced 'Vigil' silks. He moved to

Newlyn, Cornwall, in 1918, formed friendships with local artists and set up Cryséde in 1920, for the production of hand-blockprinted silks and dresses. Originally the garments were designed by Kay Earle, his wife.

Although an untrained artist, a meeting with Raoul Dufy in Paris in 1923 encouraged Walker to carry out designs derived from his own watercolour sketches of landscape. These were easily translated into blocks and printed in up to six colours. In 1925 the firm moved to St Ives, Cornwall, and the workforce expanded to 120; retailing was through Cryséde shops in Britain and by mail order to customers in Europe, Australia and America.

Designs were printed on crêpe-de-Chine, silk georgette and linen, in numerous colourways using modern synthetic dyes and pigments; they were vibrant and cheerful in colour, which accounts for their contemporary success and their great appeal today. Walker claimed that depth was achieved by "the colour being driven in with a mallet" (St Ives Times and Echo, 1925).

Walker's involvement with Cryséde ended formally in 1929 after a series of disputes, although he continued to submit designs until 1933; the company finally went into liquidation in 1941. In the years 1946-53 some of Walker's designs were reprinted in Hayle, Cornwall, by Cresta Silks.

Frank Dobson
b.1886, London, died 1963, London(?)
Dobson studied painting at the City and Guilds Art School, Kennington, London; he became a sculptor and designer. In 1914 he exhibited sculpture at the Chenil Galleries but war service interrupted his career. From 1920 he took part in exhibitions once again, including those of the London Group, of which he was president (1924-8). Dobson was also an early member of the Society of Industrial Artists, formed in 1930.

In about 1938 he entered a short phase in which he produced a series of hand-blockprinted linen furnishing fabrics, from his studio in Chelsea. Small quantities of each design exist, suggesting that they were probably made for the Dobsons' own consumption. Frank Dobson cut or carved the lino blocks and his wife Mary Dobson printed them, using ordinary printers' inks, usually one or two colours to each design. The motifs were of fishes, birds, fruit and, most unusually in textile design, the female nude – seen as Europa (with bull) or a dancer. Previously, Dobson had designed several screenprints for Allan Walton Textiles, London (1933-4).

Dobson's appointments included that of official war artist, 1940, and Professor of Sculpture at the Royal College of Art, 1946-53.

Jan Dunkley
b.1966, Yorkshire, England
Jan Dunkley studied art and design at Bretton Hall College, Yorkshire, specialising in silkscreen-printed textiles; following this she attended Huddersfield Polytechnic to prepare for associateship of the Textile Institute in design and knitted textiles. Her interest in knitted patterns then led her to Inverness where she taught the subject. After two years she achieved recognition as a chartered textile technologist of the Textile Institute.

Dunkley became keen to produce her own pattern designs and found that blockprinting with dyes would give the character and qualities she desired. In 1992 she set up a workshop to produce hand-blockprinted textiles and pattern papers in Middlesex. She is now producing her first designs for furnishing and dress fabrics from lino blocks. Much of the work is experimental and Jan Dunkley has been studying the history and practice of the subject, advised by Enid Marx (see p.46). To gain further experience, she has also worked for Ian Mortimer, the letterpress printer.

Dawn Dupree
b.1964, London, England
After attending Southwark College of Art and Goldsmith's College, London, where she studied fine art/textiles, Dawn Dupree took a short course for small businesses. In 1990 she moved into Clockwork Studios, London. In 1992 she set up in her own premises nearby, with the aid of a Crafts Council Setting-Up grant. It is significant that Dupree had already travelled the world widely during the 1980s, living in Spain and South America, and helped to make hand-painted textiles in Indonesia. Her work draws on foreign landscapes and other pictorial images in her sketchbooks; autobiographical references to her first child also occur.

Dawn Dupree is a screenprinter and hand-painter who uses the colour-discharge technique in her cotton textiles. She makes one-off hanging panels and cushions for interiors, based on drawings in oil and pastel.

These are enlarged photographically and transferred to a screen. The background cloth is usually dyed a dark colour prior to printing, then painted and discharged repeatedly.

Both textiles and drawings are sold through exhibitions and galleries.

Noel Dyrenforth
b.1936, London
Noel Dyrenforth studied painting and drawing at the Central School of Arts and Crafts and, subsequently, textiles and ceramics at Goldsmith's College and Sir John Cass, all in London.

Wishing to explore alternative artforms, he began experimenting with batik (wax-resist patterning) in 1962 and set up his first studio in London the same year. Amongst his early products were silk batik mini-dresses, which were sold successfully through Liberty's and

Woolands, London. An exhibition in 1967 at the Commonwealth Institute Art Gallery, London, established his reputation for highly coloured batiks of vigorous abstract design; examples were purchased by the Victoria and Albert Museum. Annual exhibitions followed in England and abroad.

Throughout the 1970s, at the invitation of various institutions, Dyrenforth travelled abroad extensively, teaching, leading workshops and exhibiting. In 1978 he was craftsman-in-residence to 'Arts Victoria' in Australia. At this time his work exploited the juxtaposition of distinct compositional structures and improvised techniques. The 'Aztec' series was produced and a method of pleating fabric for wall-hangings was also devised.

Interaction between cultures and the influence of special regional techniques

Left: *Jan Dunkley* Cushion Cover in 'Bracken', 1994 (detail) Cotton drill; dyed, lino-blockprinted with dye 60sq

Below: *Dawn Dupree* Cushion Cover 'Pimentos Padron', 1993 (detail) Cotton satin; dyed, screenprinted and painted with colour discharges H107 H61

Right: *Noel Dyrenforth* Panel 'Edge', 1993 (detail) Cotton; wax-resist patterned (batik) painted, dyed and discharged H127 W94

on his own ideas has been facilitated by Dyrenforth's continued travelling to teach and exhibit. In 1982 a visit to Japan introduced paste-resist and other methods to his work; trips to Indonesia and China prompted further developments. The 1980s was a period of refinement and by the end of the decade Dyrenforth described his work as "a flux of images and layers", manifested in batiks on paper, fine silk and wood veneer.

Dyrenforth has published two books: *Batik with Noel Dyrenforth*, 1975, with John Houston, and *The Technique of Batik*, 1988.

Georgina von Etzdorf
b.1955, Lima, Peru
Georgina von Etzdorf took a foundation course and a BA in textiles at Camberwell School of Art, London. Graduating in 1977, she first worked for Peppermint Design Studios (1977-8). In 1978 she started working under her own name and in 1981 formed her present partnership with Jonathan Docherty and Martin Simcock, both design graduates, who manage marketing and production.

Georgina von Etzdorf
Shawl 'Dragonfly', 1993 (detail)
Silk chiffon; screen-printed in blended colours with dyes, hand-rolled edges
L164 W109

Their original studio-workshop was a barn in Odstock, Wiltshire, where an expanded operation continues today. With a staff of 25 (excluding shops), they design, hand-screenprint, finish and market principally silk, wool and rayon fabrics, producing two fashion collections a year of men's and women's clothing and accessories. In addition, the firm has a second design studio and two shops in London, a concession in Barneys in New York and an international market.

Georgina von Etzdorf is the principal designer, helped by two assistants and a design developer. Watercolour and gouache paintings form the basis of the patterns and a personal style of fluid brush strokes and dynamic movement is apparent. These are put into repeat in the studio and then converted into colour separations for screen-making by an outside contractor. Luxurious ground cloths are purchased internationally; these are sampled in different colourways using the firm's palette of 2000 acid and reactive dyes. All printing and finishing is carried out in-house, with the exception of some velvets; cutting and sewing is done by outworkers.

In addition, von Etzdorf has been a visiting lecturer at colleges of art and the recipient of many small business awards and nominations.

Footprints – Joyce Clissold
b.1905, Scarborough, Yorkshire, England; died 1982, London
Joyce Clissold attended classes in design, wood-engraving, lino-cutting and printing in the School of Book Production at the Central School of Arts and Crafts (1927-9). Whilst still a student, she began work at the Footprints textile printing workshop, owned by Celandine Kennington and then in Hammersmith Terrace.

Clissold took over the workshop in 1929 and from then onwards was the designer of the textiles. Cloth was printed by wood and lino blocks, sometimes with the addition of stencilling. A team of girls, led by Cicely Swingler, carried out the orders. In c.1934 Footprints moved to Brentford, Middlesex, and occupied part of Joyce Clissold's home; a financial partner joined the business. Footprints shops were opened at 94

New Bond Street in 1933 (transferred to No.110A in 1936), and 22 Knightsbridge in 1935; these prospered until c.1940.

The workshop produced dress fabrics (silks, cottons, rayon and, later, nylon) in a range of colourways which could be ordered in the shops for making up as clothes; finished garments and georgette scarves were also on sale. The printing was frequently carried out on cut-out garment pieces for which quite small blocks were used with great freedom. Unusual grounds for

banners (or flags) of geometric design for fashion shows, as well as doing experimental work with a deliberately restricted range of dyes and discharges. This produced the characteristic near-monochrome palette seen in her work of the 1980s.

Greaves-Lord set up her first workshop in London in 1982, with the help of a Crafts Council Setting-Up Grant; at this time she combined executing painted interiors (shops and recording studios) with making individual textiles for exhibition or to commission. Her large-scale work led to her appointment, in 1985, as creative director to the Issey Miyake fashion shops in the UK and, in the '90s, to commissions for site-specific banners, sets for television programmes, sculptures and screens.

Greaves-Lord worked from four different London workshops before moving, in 1991, to North Yorkshire and setting up a studio in her cottage. She now paints and screenprints large commissions, textiles for her own collection, a few scarves and special small designs on silk, destined for reproduction as graphics by Issey Miyake, Tokyo. The imagery, although still abstract, is derived from the landscape and is more complex and colourful than formerly.

Above:
Sally Greaves-Lord
Two Samples for the
Issey Miyake
'Permanente'
Autumn/Winter
collection, 1992/3
Spun silk; painted with
dyes and discharge
front and back
Largest L32 W33

Left:
Footprints – Joyce Clissold
Triangular Scarf 'Loop
and Rope', 1948-50
(detail) Silk georgette;
blockprinted with dyes
on undyed ground;
piqué edges L134
Mrs Nancy Babbage

printing up as dress materials were favoured by Clissold although furnishing linens were also produced, some of which were subcontracted to a silkscreen-printer, after the war.

Clissold's designs frequently illustrate events and places; her fondness for the landscape – which she explored, taking watercolours and sketchbook – and for animals is apparent throughout her singular and humorous pre-War work. After c.1948 she turned to printing household items and scarves, sold mainly at county and other

shows, and to making collages; this she continued until her death in 1982.

Sally Greaves-Lord
b.1957, Sutton Coldfield, England
An art school education at Bournville School of Art & Crafts (Birmingham), West Surrey College of Art and Design, and the Royal College of Art (graduated 1982) has provided Sally Greaves-Lord with an ability to work on one-off textiles for many applications.

Whilst still a student, she sold designs for printed textiles and painted cotton

Diana Harrison
Hanging Panel, 1993
Silk; dyed, machine-
quilted, screenprinted
with discharge, painted
with gold pigment 85sq

Diana Harrison

b.1950, London, England
Harrison studied in London taking a Dip. AD course in embroidery at Goldsmith's College and then an MA in printed textiles at the Royal College of Art. Since graduation in 1973 she has taught continuously in art colleges and is currently a lecturer at West Surrey College of Art and Design.

As a student, Harrison made printed and sprayed individual cloth works rather than designing yardage in repeat. In her first workshop, at '401½', a group studio in a south London warehouse, she translated her ideas into optical-patterned furnishings. Production consisted of machine-quilted sofa and bed-coverings, cushions and wall-hangings, in satin acetate coloured by spray-gun.

In the 1980s Harrison continued working with multi-layered cloth and applied colour by splattering and spraying. Leading on from these, the monochrome works of the 1990s have the same basic construction but use different fibres and dye methods. The multi-layered fabric is machine-stitched, dyed, discharge-printed and over-printed repeatedly; this gives the impression of the passage of time.

It is important for Harrison to develop her ideas through drawing and design, calculating the composition and pattern before embarking on a piece. She now concentrates on making, from her studio at home, one-off, experimental 'quilts', which are mainly for exhibition. Works are included in public collections at the Crafts Council, Embroiderers' Guild, the Victoria and Albert Museum and the Museum of Modern Art, Kyoto.

Enid Marx, RDI

b.1902, London
Enid Marx printed her first scarf, inspired by Japanese cut paper stencils, while a schoolgirl at Roedean, Sussex. After training as a painter at the Royal College of Art in the 1920s, she worked for Barron and Larcher's London textile printing workshop for a year in 1925. The

work was laborious but she learnt the rudiments and recipes of her craft. At the same point she designed her first pattern paper for Curwen Press.

Enid Marx set up her first of a series of four workshops in Hampstead in 1926, and worked almost single-handedly until 1939. Producing hand-blockprinted textiles was her main occupation for 14 years but ceased with the outbreak of World War II and the scarcity of materials.

Marx cut her own printing blocks, using hardwood or linoleum mounted on wood, sometimes with the addition of metal pins, which printed as dots. The fabrics used for printing were cotton, organdie, linen and velveteen, with which Marx had a great affinity. She enjoyed the limitations of colour derived from natural dyes such as indigo, rust and iron.

The patterns are deceptively simple and ingenious, mostly abstract repeating motifs, sometimes using rotations of the same block to create tumbling and wave effects. Floral subjects also appear, informed by Enid Marx's interest in gardening. Painting – her own and other artists' work – together with primitive textiles have also influenced her designs.

Marx also received important commissions for woven textile designs: seating fabric for the London Underground (1937) and for the Utility Furniture scheme (1944). Her full *oeuvre* includes wood-engraving and auto-lithography for pattern papers, book illustration and book jackets, postage stamps, writing on English popular art, in conjunction with her friend Margaret Lambert, and teaching.

Above: *Enid Marx* Length of 'Shooting star' (No.11), 1930s (detail) Organdie; blockprinted with dyes on an undyed ground L212 W108

Right: *Bettina Mitchell* Square, 1990 (detail) Fine silk; dyed and discharged ground, stencilled and screenprinted with dye L93 W88

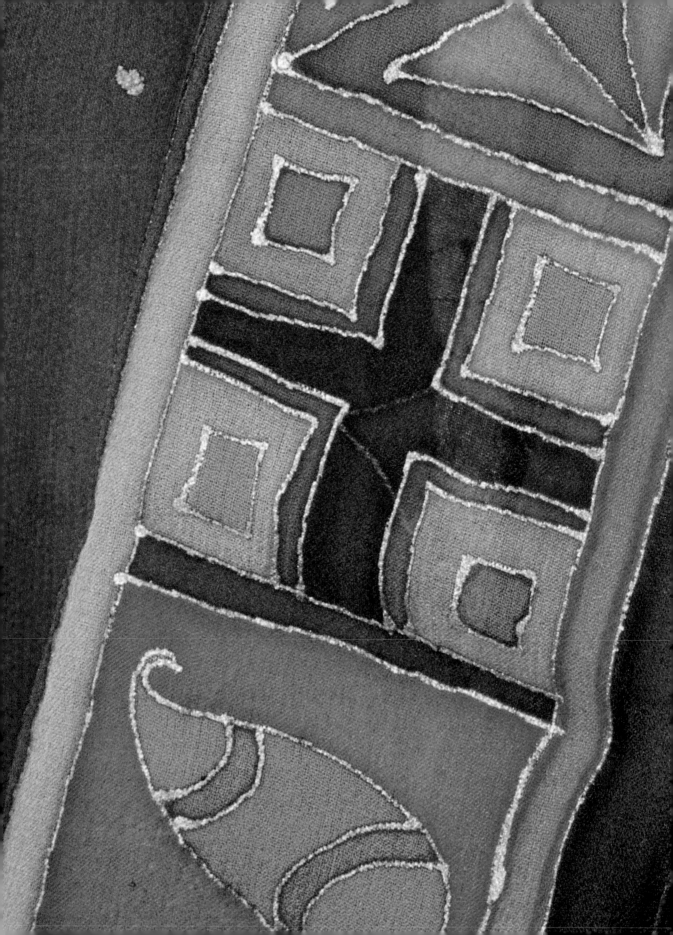

Bettina Mitchell

b.1965, Gloucester, England

Bettina Mitchell studied tapestry and printed textiles at Central St Martin's College of Art and Design, and set up a workshop at the South Bank Craft Centre, London, in 1989. Working alone she combines screenprinting, painting and stencilling on silk and devoré velvet, producing scarves and cushions.

Mitchell's designs centre around the subject of music, musicians and their instruments; many of these are derived from her pen and ink drawings worked in situ at the Festival Hall. She also uses elements from illuminated manuscripts. These are translated photographically into line images and amalgamated with hand-painted and stencilled areas on the cloth.

In 1993 Bettina Mitchell returned to Central St Martin's and began studying for a Masters degree in printed textiles; she is exploring textile printing in developing countries and hopes eventually to teach her craft abroad.

Sarbjit Natt

b.1962, India

Sarbjit Natt attended four colleges, taking her main textile/fashion BTech diploma at Cleveland College of Art and Design in 1985; she then studied at the London College of Furniture. She was awarded an RSA bursary in 1985 and a Prince's Trust Award in 1987. On leaving college she worked as a commercial embroidery designer and since 1991 has run her silk-painting workshop at the Selby Centre, north London, where she also teaches.

Her silk accessories – scarves, handkerchieves, hats, hairbands and cushions – are decorative but not fashion-led. The technique is her own; the complex patterns are first drawn freehand with a textile marker on the silk; this line disappears under the dyes. A rubber-based metallic outline, known as 'gutta', is painted on the fabric while damp. Colour is painted on, inside the lines, and steamed to fix. Natt refers to the many colours, mixed from a basis of ten, as "spiced up to bring forward the flavour of India". The patterns draw on Phulkarie and Bagh embroideries as their source.

Natt takes part in workshops, exhibitions and craft fairs throughout the country to teach and sell her work.

Trisha Needham

b.1961, Leeds, England

After training in textiles at West Surrey College of Art and Design and the Royal College of Art, Trisha Needham graduated in 1985. She began her career by teaching at West Surrey and at Harrow School of Art, making use of the workshop facilities at the latter. In 1988 she moved into a studio-workshop at Clockwork Studios, alongside other designers and artists. Needham produces abstract-patterned fashion shawls and scarves, enjoying the discipline of the square or the rectangle; she works in two fibres. On wool she carries out two separate techniques: directly hand-painting or, alternatively, dyeing the cloth then painting or printing on a discharge paste. When printing she uses a small screen, moved about freely. On silk georgette or chiffon she adopts a conventional screenprinting method to achieve repeating patterns of up to six colours on a cream ground. Specialising in design for sheer fabrics, Needham has undertaken a large commission for cotton organdie curtains for the Education Funding Council building in Bristol.

Far Left: *Sabjit Natt Long Scarf, 'Amargit'* 1993 (detail) Silk georgette, drawn gutta-resist, painted with dyes; hand-rolled edges L215 W116

Opposite: *Trisha Needham Square, 'Doughnuts',* 1987 (detail) Wool; dyed, discharge-screenprinted and painted 132sq

Below: *EQ Nicholson Rectangular Scarf, 'Tigers',* c.1928 Silk; wax-resist patterned and dyed H79 W91.5 Timothy Nicholson

E.Q. Nicholson

b.1908, London; died 1992, London

After spending only three weeks at the Slade, E.Q., as she was known, spent six months in Paris in 1926 learning the art of batik (wax-resist) painting on silk. This she put into practice working in London for Marion Dorn, the textile and carpet designer.

In 1931 E.Q. (neé Myers) married the architect Kit Nicholson and from c.1936 began to collaborate with him on interiors using her designs on cotton fabrics, which she printed by lino-block. In this decade she also made ambitious, individual batik furnishings and scarves, featuring animals, and worked experimentally combining stencilling, stippling and painting on fabric.

By the 1940s she had turned increasingly to painting but also contributed designs for commercial silkscreen printing to Edinburgh Weavers and, in the 1950s, sold wallpaper designs to Cole and Son. E.Q. Nicholson resumed textile activity in the 1980s when she designed scarves and made hooked wool rugs based on her own designs and those of her son, Tim Nicholson.

Nancy Nicholson

b.1899, Woodstock, Oxfordshire; died 1977, London

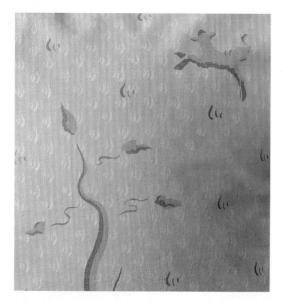

Nancy Nicholson, daughter of the artists William Nicholson and Mabel Pryde, had no formal art training; she became an illustrator and later a fabric printer. In 1918 she married the poet Robert Graves and lived for a short time in North Wales and then in Oxfordshire. Following their separation, Nancy Nicholson set up Poulk Prints, also operating as the Poulk Press, in Wiltshire in 1929. The workshop produced lino-block prints on cotton, possibly using printers' inks, in patterns mostly to her design and also to her brother Ben Nicholson's. The Press settled finally at Sutton Veny, Wiltshire, where its most important commission was furnishings, as well as interior colour schemes, for Laugharne Castle.

Most of Nancy Nicholson's designs date from before 1939 and characteristically combine a single stencilled motif with a repeating pattern; she continued to print them in the 1940s, '50s and '60s. In 1945 she moved the Poulk Press to a studio-shop in London's Belgravia, where she printed on the premises and displayed her fabrics. In the last years of her life, and for a few years after her death,

Nancy Nicholson's daughter-in-law, Annelise Graves, reprinted the blocks on cushion covers.

Pazuki Prints – Pookie Blezard

b.1960, London, England

Pookie Blezard and Suzy Thompson, partners in Pazuki until 1993, both studied printed textiles at Camberwell School of Art and Crafts. Following graduation in 1982, they set up the partnership with the help of the Enterprise Allowance Scheme. At first they designed and screenprinted scarves and lengths of fashion fabric in their own studio – the loft of a large London house. Their designs were experimental and showed two distinct hands at work.

Pazuki's studio became too small as the business expanded and now all the printing is subcontracted and the products made by outworkers all over England. Ninety per cent of sales are exported to fashion outlets throughout the world. The partnership was dissolved recently but Pookie Blezard continues to design the textiles and run the business.

Victoria Richards

b.1964, Exeter, England

After taking a foundation course at Exeter College of Art and Design, Victoria Richards attended West Surrey College of Art and Design, graduating in 1985. Her first workshop was set up in 1986, aided by a Crafts Council grant, at Clockwork Studios, London. In 1985 she was awarded a place on the graduate enterprise programme, Cranfield University, Bedfordshire, and in 1990 a grant from the Prince's Trust to investigate business partnerships in Europe. With the latter she travelled to Italy.

Georgina Scott
Rectangular Wrap,
1991 (detail)
Linen; painted with dye, bound and dyed in indigo, over-dyed in K-salt; masked and discharged; burnished finish L160 w45

Richards is a screenprinter and discharge-printer whose designs develop organically by use of one screen which is moved or rotated on the cloth; she frequently over-dyes at different stages of production. The fabrics employed are silks and silk-satins, velvet, lycra and damask.

She is closely involved with the fashion market for both individual prints and designs on fabrics, which are sold to couture houses with whom she works closely.

In addition, Victoria Richards teaches on the foundation course at Wimbledon School of Art and contributes to special programmes at Cranfield University.

Georgina Scott

b.1968, Leeds, England

Following a foundation course at York College of Arts and Technology, Georgina Scott graduated in textiles from West Surrey College of Art and Design. She set up her workshop in a garage at her home in Farnham in 1991, and combines textile-making with a job in a carpet gallery. She also teaches introductory courses on all aspects of dyeing at Guildhall University, London, and has taught resist-dyeing to students at West Surrey College.

The area in which Georgina Scott specialises is resist-dyeing, particularly of linen and silk. After masking-out or pleating her cloth lengthways, she binds it with fine threads, using rotating tubes on a specially designed machine. She dyes, then over-dyes the cloth, and sometimes bleaches out defined areas by brushing on a discharge paste. Indigo and K-salt are favourite dyestuffs.

Scott works chiefly to commission and has produced a kimono for the collection at Nagoya Museum, Japan, for the International Shibori Symposium (1992).

Margaret Simeon

b.1910, London

Margaret Simeon trained at Chelsea School of Art from 1926 to 1930, then attended the Royal College of Art, graduating in 1935. She was awarded the RCA Travelling Scholarship in 1934.

Throughout her career Simeon worked from her home at Clapham Common, London, as a freelance designer of woven and printed furnishing and dress fabrics. Some of the prints she executed herself by hand-block and screen, but she is perhaps better known for designs for machine-printed textiles and wallpapers, produced by firms including Allan Walton Textiles, Campbell Fabrics, Edinburgh Weavers, Fortnum & Mason, Heal's, Helios, Warner Fabrics and John Lewis, in the period c.1935-1970. Many of these originated as hand-prints and were sold as design-prototypes on cloth.
(see illustration p.8-9)

Norma Starszakowna

b.1945, Fife, Scotland

In 1966 Starszakowna received a Dip.AD from Duncan of Jordanstone College of Art, Dundee, where she is now course director for textiles and deputy head of the School of Design. On completing her education she was awarded a place at the Royal College of Art but instead opted to set up her own studio-workshop in Dundee.

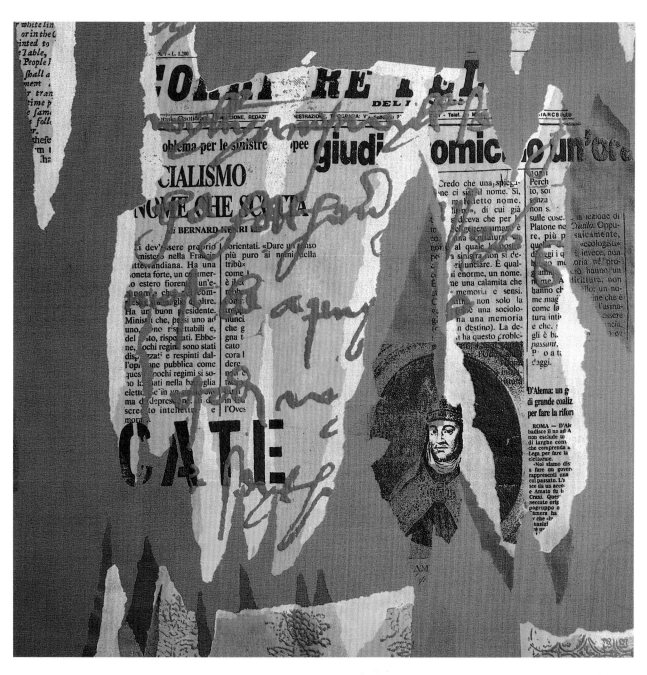

As a textile designer-maker Starszakowna operates in two different areas: one-off batik panels and hand-screenprinted yardage in repeat. Her Habotai silk batiks employ fine, detailed drawing in tones and layers of colours, creating spatial effects; these are exhibited internationally.

Amongst her recent fashion fabrics are textured, raised and embossed examples using hand-printing, varnish and pigment processes. This work

began in 1977 when Starszakowna received a Scottish Arts Council Research Award and developed as part of the proposed Winchester Cathedral Textiles Project; samples were selected by the designer Issey Miyake for use as vestments and processional banners. Starszakowna is currently working on new dye and print processes, for one-off, free-hanging banners.

Lesley Sunderland

b.1947, Henley-on-Thames, England
Sunderland studied printed textiles at Chelsea School of Art and the Royal College of Art, graduating in 1971. She lived in Los Angeles in 1971-2 and there produced a series of hand-painted, sculpted leather gloves; these were exhibited in London in 1975. From 1972 to '84 Sunderland taught surface design at Chelsea.

Norma Starszakowna
Length of Furnishing Fabric, 1993 (detail)
Silk organza; dyed and screenprinted with pigments and spandex medium
W107.5 L269

Above:
Lesley Sunderland
Length of 'Rococo',
1986 (detail)
Cotton; wood-
blockprinted with dyes
on a painted ground
L152 W137.5

Sunderland moved to Wales in 1975, adapted to new studio conditions and began undertaking commissions for bespoke furnishings embracing many period styles. The works – lengths, window and door surrounds, bed-hangings and curtains, furniture coverings, wall-hangings and screens – are either hand-painted or block-printed, or employ a combination of the two techniques.

Furnishing lengths are worked 'by the piece' on the print table, frequently printing onto a wet, brush-dyed ground to produce dramatic effect. The printing blocks are carved from lime wood or mahogany by Sunderland's partner, Jonathan Heale, and the dyes employed are Procions and pigments; painted details can be applied by bristle brush. The ground cloths are cotton sateen, linen and canvas.

The motifs found in Sunderland's individual painted textiles are frequently realistic flowers or leaves, worked in colours to suit a particular piece of furniture or interior. Textile furnishings for complete interiors can also be supplied by the studio.

Marianne de Trey
b.1913, London, of Swiss parentage
Marianne de Trey studied textile design under Reco Capey at the Royal College of Art; here she worked in tie-and-die, wax-resist, lino-blockprinted and painted techniques. Following graduation in 1935 she taught textile design and printing at Ipswich School of Art.

In 1939 de Trey left England with her husband, the potter Sam Haile, and lived in the USA during the war years. Whilst in America she produced and sold designs for commercially printed

fabrics, but ceased to design or make textiles on her return to England.

Marianne de Trey turned to pottery from c.1945, moved to Dartington, Devon, in 1947 and re-established the Shinner's Bridge Pottery there that year. Her tin-glazed earthenware, dating from the early 1950s, shows clearly her training as a pattern designer and colourist. She continued running the pottery during the 1960s and early '70s and now operates her own small workshop adjacent to Dartington Pottery, where she makes individual porcelain pots.

Sharon May Yee Peng Ting
b.1968, Surrey, England
In summer 1992 Ting graduated in printed textiles from the Royal College of Art; she had previously studied at West Surrey College of Art and Design and Wimbledon School of Art. During her student years she received the Worshipful Company of Haber-dasher's prize (1991), took two prizes at the 1992 Texprint Interstoff Fabric Fair and was awarded a judges' commendation for textiles in the 1992 Pantone European Colour Awards.

Sharon Ting's designs for commercially printed textiles have been sold to textile companies internationally, but she now concentrates on the craft area of production. In her shared Holborn? workshop, for which she received a Crafts Council Setting-Up Grant, she makes fashion accessories and lengths together with hanging panels or banners, for specific interiors.

Ting uses painting and hand-screenprinting in combination; she also employs the techniques of discharge and devoré. Her patterns, often grid-like, are the result of adding and subtracting colour in alternating operations; this has produced certain effects which are virtually unrepeatable.

Sian Tucker

b.1958, Norwich, England
Following art school courses at Lincoln (1976-7), Middlesex (1977-80) and the Royal College of Art (1980-2), Sian Tucker immediately set up her own workshop with the assistance of a Crafts Council Setting-Up Grant.

She then started painting directly onto fabrics, mainly wools, with acid dyes, and steamed them in a small boiler. In the main, she painted scarves which were bought by UK retailers as designs for reproduction, in the same way as designs on paper; many were sold in this way. Concurrently, she painted one-off scarves, fabrics for garments, screens and hanging panels. The early range of designs was devoted to geometrics in primary colours but gradually altered by the mid-1980s to include a broader range and simple figurative images often arranged against geometric backgrounds.

In 1988 Tucker moved to a larger studio, shared with Sally Greaves-Lord (see p.43); her techniques for textile painting remained unaltered but she took the decision to concentrate on obtaining commissions, in particular for public areas. The most prestigious of these, for the new Chelsea and Westminster Hospital, is a 75-foot-high mobile consisting of over 80 highly coloured elements, together with six complementary painted hangings.

Over the 11 year period, Tucker's work has embraced many areas of mass-market surface design: stationery and wrapping paper, ceramics, tinware and book illustration. Hand-knotted rugs, made to her designs, have also been produced in Turkey.

Carole Waller

b.1956, Birmingham, England
Carole Waller attended Bournville School of Art and Crafts, Birmingham, and Canterbury College of Art, where she studied fine art/painting. After two years working as a gallery assistant, she went to Cranbrook Academy of Art, USA, to study fine art/fibres. On her return in 1986 she occupied one of the spaces at Winchester Design Workshops, for graduates. Here she researched dyes and equipment, and made painted clothes under the name 'I'm No Walking Canvas'. After leaving Winchester, Waller built a studio in Southampton, using a Southern Arts grant. She worked alone until 1993, when she moved her home and studio to Bath and took on a studio assistant.

Most of Waller's designs are descriptive, evoking a place or event by the use of superimposed images. Her technique employs dyes, screenprinted and freely painted onto silk and cotton, in arrangements suitable for the cut of each garment. She also makes painting and installations, sometimes collaborating with performing artists. About 300 pieces are produced in her workshop annually, made to commission or sold through shops and galleries in England and abroad.